Der

KU-488-447

THE BOOK OF SHIPS

Idea, design and text © 1968.
Tre Tryckare, Cagner & Co.
Gothenburg, Sweden.

Illustrations by Tre Tryckare artists except sailing ships by Gordon Macfie.

Printed in Holland by Smeets Photo-Offset, Weert.

First published in Great Britain in 1968 by Macdonald and Co. (Publishers) Ltd.
Gulf House,
2 Portman Street,
London W.1.

2

CLASSICS OF TRANSPORTATION

the book of
SHIPS

by
Laurence Dunn

MACDONALD : LONDON

ILLUSTRATIONS   Page

Man's present efforts to achieve mastery of the element of air merely echo, in essence, the earlier battle waged over almost countless centuries to gain the freedom of that other element, the sea. There was, however, one essential difference that moulded the pattern of development; the material to voyage on water was ready to hand in wood, whose relative lightness makes it buoyant. For it must have been on some solid log or bough that early man first experienced travel afloat.

How long an interval of time elapsed between the first precarious journeys astride some floating piece of wood and the hollowing of the first tree trunk is something we will never know. But had not wood been inherently buoyant many more centuries might have elapsed before man achieved the idea of a flotation solely dependent on hollowness.

Often in the study of any development—for example that of the early steam engine—the historian discovers afresh instances of contemporary parallels of thought, even in widely separated parts of the world. Even so, from the early days of inter-tribal trading there would also be a like spread of ideas. If travel by river was involved then there must

have been eager scrutiny of the craft used by the visiting traders.

Our knowledge of early seagoing craft is full of gaps, and it is of those of the Eastern Mediterranean that we have the most information. Even so, representations of these are so stylised as to make accurate interpretation difficult. Although centuries apart, Egyptian and Roman craft were representative of an early diversity in concept, largely due to the materials available.

The shaping of Egyptian boats reflected that country's lack of suitable timber. Evolved from rafts woven of papyrus reeds, they were shallow and spoon-shaped, their length about four times their breadth. Such wood as was available—generally acacia—came in small pieces. The result was a lack of longitudinal strength and this was remedied by the use of a truss stretched high above the hull, its ends attached to the bow and stern. Other characteristic fittings were a large steering oar and a squaresail, although oarsmen provided the real motive power.

Characteristic of the Mediterranean by contrast, was the galley, and it remained long in vogue, but with its slim lines and many oarsmen it had little room for cargo. By about the time of Christ local trading needs, notably the carriage of corn, had resulted in a full-lined sailing ship, not unlike the Roman vessel shown. Although robust, these were nevertheless difficult to handle.

Since ancient times the two common methods of fastening planking to the hulls of wooden vessels have been the clinker and carvel. In the former the planks overlap, while in the latter—a style born in the Mediterranean—the planks are laid flat, edge to edge.

Since the Viking age the Nordic ship, in its basic design—though modified in detail to suit local needs—was an undecked craft with an oak clinker-built hull. Low amidships, but ending in a tall slim bow and stern, these vessels were very manoeuvrable and could sail surprisingly close to the wind. A representative Nordic ship of intermediate size was 77 ft. long and 17 ft. broad.

By the beginning of the Middle Ages the types used in Northern Europe were undergoing considerable change, their shapes influenced by those of Western and Southern Europe. Low, undecked vessels gave way to something taller, with a lofty castle at each end. When fighting took place it was generally at very close quarters and merchantmen so shaped were less vulnerable to attack and boarding. Although their height and full lines

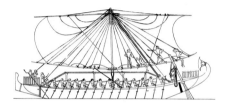

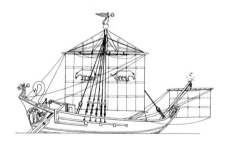

A large Egyptian ship of 1600 B.C. and (below) a Roman trading vessel of 200 A.D. There is much similarity between the latter and existing Turkish caiques of the present day.

7

made them unhandy and difficult to sail in anything but a fair wind, they depended on sails rather than on oarsmen.

The triangular lateen sail had been introduced in the Mediterranean by the Arabs in the eighth century, and from that time on it was much used for small vessels. In Spain and Portugal these small ones were known as caravels, while larger ones were called naos. Of Columbus' fleet the SANTA MARIA was a nao and the little, fast-sailing NINA a caravel.

Superstructure apart, the hulls of these and the Norman vessels were not so very dissimilar in profile, but in the former the islands had become an integral part of the hull. The poop, wide at its after edge, was now a dominant feature with a rudder in place of the old steering oar. But with respect to sails, there were great changes and the use of the lateen aided steering and so brought greater handiness.

The nao had two extra sails; a very tapered topsail carried above the fighting top and a spritsail (or blinde) set beneath that still relatively new spar, the bowsprit. Another new development affected the mainsail, which was no longer in one part. Instead, low down, there were two detachable

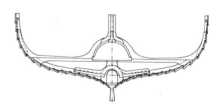

Up to the present time, the largest, and most intact, of all Viking ships ever discovered was found in 1880 at Gokstad on the western shore of the Oslo Fjord. A cross section of the Gokstad ship, which dates from about the year 850-950 A.D., is seen above.

8

sections called bonnets. In bad weather these could be removed, a great improvement over contemporary reefing.

Throughout the sixteenth and seventeenth centuries the pattern was one of gradual evolution, affecting both hull shape and sails. In particular, the forward island—born as a fighting platform—underwent great change.

Its height was reduced and it was stepped back from the bows. There a beak was developed and the bowsprit given more prominence. On this extra headsails provided much needed compensation for the still unduly high poop which offered great wind resistance.

Guns had been carried since the middle of the fourteenth century. Their use was not confined to warships. Merchantmen, for their very survival, were often defensively armed. Originally small guns had been carried on the top deck or castles, but in 1501 a Frenchman named Descharges, from Brest, conceived the idea of cutting ports in the sides of the hull and placing them on a lower deck. Stability was immediately improved and so larger ships and guns became possible. Older vessels had been characterised by great height in relation to length and by excessive sheer, the

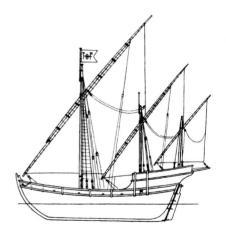

A Spanish caravel of about 1490, a smaller vessel which, in this instance, has lateen sails only.

9

curvature of the hull from bow to stern. By making the gun deck more nearly straight and horizontal this area was made more efficient and gradually the new arrangement led to a reduction in poop height.

Long distance trade to the Indies which had been developed by Portugal and Spain during the Renaissance was subsequently followed by that of the great trading companies formed in Britain, Holland and Sweden. In the ships needed for such voyages the emphasis was on strength and cargo capacity rather than speed. Even so, masts were made progressively taller and were fashioned in several sections, the lower mast being given a topmast and above this a topgallant mast, these two giving their names to the sails they carried. The lateen, aft, had long since been reshaped and become known as the driver or spanker, while staysails, set between the masts, became usual. The spread of canvas was further increased by extra sails aloft, royals becoming common over the topgallant sails, skysails sometimes being carried too. The width of canvas was likewise increased, by the use of stunsails extending outward from the lower yards on either side.

While the steamboat was being developed, sail reached its climax in the clipper, of

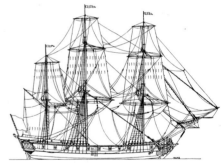

An English caravel of about 1500 and a large Swedish frigate of 1768. Note the development of topsails and great reduction in poop height.

which one, the American SOVEREIGN OF THE SEAS proved capable of 22 knots—the fastest sailer ever. However, the opening of the Suez Canal in 1869 ended the supremacy of sail and from then on emphasis became progressively more centred on economy and the use of smaller crews, this leading to such simplified rigs as the barque and schooner.

American nineteenth century pre-eminence at sea was shortlived, due large to the reluctance of American builders to forsake wooden hulls and sail. Higher insurance rates resulting from the Civil War also led to the sale of many ships. The schooner, attractive because of its handiness and crew economy, originated in the United States. Initially two-masted, it developed into something very much larger, and many multi-masted schooners were built for the American coal and timber trades. Probably the most important were those employed along the U.S. Eastern seaboard. There some 300 four-masted schooners were built over the period from 1890 to 1910. Many others had five, some six and one even seven masts. The WYOMING, the last of the great coal schooners, was launched in 1909, but by 1919 her type was virtually extinct, at least in America.

A typical barque of 1865. Note how, compared with the previous ship, the topsails and topgallant sails have been divided, this for greater ease in handling.

In Northern Europe, especially Scandinavia, the schooner—of small to medium size—had a long run of popularity. Unlike the big Americans, they often carried one or more squaresails on the foremast. In early days even small schooners made long ocean voyages, carrying fruit or salted fish, but later the type became more confined to the short sea trades, timber being an important cargo. By the second world war the European schooner had almost disappeared.

It is obvious that in one sense sail was preceded by mechanically propelled vessels. The simplest form of mechanical propulsion—the strength of man applied through paddles or oars—served to move war and cargo ships of the ancient and medieval world. Large crews of oarsmen and the stores to feed them severely restricted the cargo capacity of vessels so propelled. Warships required oars for rapid manoeuvring but in oar-driven merchantmen cargo space was at so high a premium that only valuable goods such as silk and spice could be carried. Even in early history ordinary bulky cargoes were relegated to the relatively slow but capacious sailing vessels.

Other means of mechanical propulsion were also tried out. Before the Christian era paddle

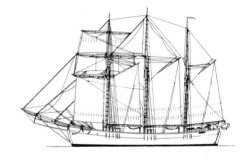

A North European, three-masted topsail schooner—a very versatile type—and below, a large six-master, typical of those used on the U.S. East Coast.

wheels turned by oxen propelled some of the boats used to carry the Roman Legions of Claudius Caudex to Sicily. A bas-relief of about A.D. 527 showed a war vessel having three pairs of paddle wheels, each turned by two oxen. On the opposite side of the world Chinese sources mention man-propelled paddle-wheels on warships of the 7th, 12th and 16th centuries. A manuscript of 1430 in Munich describes a warship fitted with four paddle-wheels mounted on crank-shafts turned by four men, while later in that century Leonardo da Vinci sketched many other propulsion schemes.

In England, Thomas Newcomen completed a successful atmospheric engine in 1705, and this early steam engine was soon widely used for pumping out coal and tin mines. Marquis Claude de Jouffroy d'Abbans is generally accepted as being the first successful pioneer in the marine application of steam power. His second boat, the PYROSCAPHE, when tried on the Saone river in 1783 proved briefly able to travel against the current. After the Revolution he built another, the CHARLES PHILIPPE, and this he operated on the Seine.

Already experienced with paddles driven by man or beast, Patrick Miller of Glasgow enlisted the aid of William Symington—then working on a steam carriage—who built an engine which had two vertical Newcomen atmospheric cylinders. These he installed in one hull of a twin-hulled boat, fitting a boiler in the other hull. Placed in tandem between the hulls were two chain-driven paddle wheels. On trials in 1788 the boat, which measured 25 ft. long by 7 ft. wide, achieved a speed of about 5 miles an hour. A year later another boat fitted with similar machinery was successfully tried on the Forth & Clyde Canal in Scotland.

In America the summer of 1790 saw John Fitch's EXPERIMENT successfully carrying passengers between New York, Trenton and intermediate towns. That season she made in all 14 trips—some 2,000 miles—with only a few breakdowns. Even so, the venture proved a financial failure and Fitch's company soon collapsed. His EXPERIMENT was propelled by three "duck leg" paddles at the stern which were operated by cranks and rods from a horizontal shaft fitted across the square stern. The engine was geared to a shaft fitted with sprocket wheels, a chain or rope drive transmitting power to the stern shaft and so to the paddles. Steam was provided by a so-called pipe or tubular boiler in which the hot gases passed through tubes surrounded by water.

Of other early efforts the Scottish-built CHARLOTTE DUNDAS of 1801 was the most notable and was, indeed, probably the first practical steamboat. She was designed to replace the horses which towed barges on the Forth & Clyde Canal and this she did with success; nevertheless fears that her wash might damage the canal banks caused her to be soon laid aside. Her wooden hull had a single paddlewheel in a covered stern recess. The double stern so formed had twin rudders controlled from near the bows.

The next major development again took place in America, where Robert Fulton and Robert R. Livingston built a boat which secured for them the monopoly of New York waters. About her there is much conflicting evidence; instead of being named CLERMONT as was long believed, it seems more likely that she was called the NORTH RIVER. Her hull, built at New York, was given a 20 h.p. engine imported from England. This had a vertical cylinder 24 in. in diameter and with a 4 ft. stroke which drove two paddle-wheels. Steam was provided by an externally fired copper boiler mounted on bricks. In her design Fulton showed his genius in being

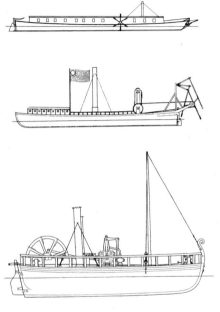

Early experimental steamboats: Jouffroy's PYROSCAPHE of 1783, John Fitch's EXPERIMENT (1788) which had "duck leg" paddles, and the CHARLOTTE DUNDAS of 1801.

able first to consolidate the ideas of earlier inventors and then to keep on introducing refinements.

The NORTH RIVER made her first run from New York to Albany and back in August 1807. Several times rebuilt, she was successfully employed on the Hudson until 1814. There, by 1810, Fulton had two other steamboats in service, while a year later he designed the first one to operate on the Mississippi. Simultaneously in Britain, the COMET introduced a passenger service on the Clyde and so stimulated interest that by 1815 ten steam packets were plying on that river alone.

From then on the use of steamboats spread through Europe. Once their practicality on short routes was proved, the next challenge was to make them capable of long ocean voyages. The ENTERPRISE, built at Deptford in 1824, was intended for service to and from India. A three-masted vessel with a full set of canvas, she could do 8 knots under steam alone. Although she proved hardly suitable for her purpose, she successfully completed a voyage to Calcutta, where she was sold to give many years of useful service. Another vessel, launched a year earlier at Dover, was sold to become the CURACAO,

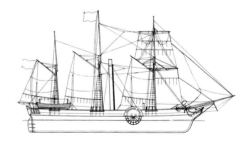

The COMET, built for Clyde service in 1812 and (below) the FERDINANDO PRIMO of 1818, the first steamer to operate in the Mediterranean. She lasted only two years in this service.

15

the first steamer in the Netherlands Navy; by 1830 she had several trans-Atlantic voyages to her credit.

Of the early ocean-going ships, the GREAT WESTERN was the first full-powered steamer designed for regular trans-Atlantic service which actually was to achieve that end. The impact of her first appearance at New York in 1838 was lessened by the prior arrival—also from England—of the SIRIUS. In contrast to this small chartered vessel which made only two round voyages, the GREAT WESTERN was employed on the Atlantic until 1850.

The year 1840 saw the opening of a regular passenger service between England and Alexandria, as well as the completion of the BRITANNIA, the first of a quartette for Mr. Samuel Cunard and with which he started a regular twice-monthly trans-Atlantic service. For many years the use of paddle-wheels and wooden hulls remained the rule; in America over-long retention of the latter contributed to the subsequent decline of her merchant fleet. The next major developments were the introduction of the screw propeller and of specialised types, of which the steam collier was one.

The superiority of the screw propeller was

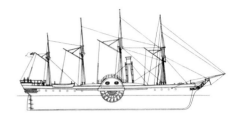

The GREAT WESTERN (1837) spent 12 years on trans-Atlantic service. The JOHN BOWES, of 1852, was the first full-powered screw collier and bore many names before being lost at sea in 1933.

16

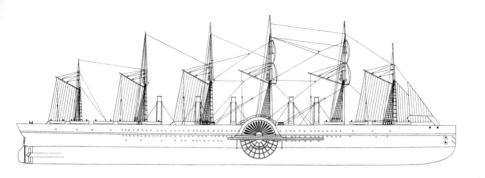

ably demonstrated in 1839 by the small British steamer ARCHIMEDES. This led to a change of plan for Britain's next major ship, the GREAT BRITAIN, which was completed as a propeller steamer, not paddle as originally intended. She was the first large iron ship to be built, also the first screw-propelled steamer to cross the Atlantic. Typical of the times, her boiler pressure was very low, only 15 p.s.i. Even so, she did over 11 knots on trial. The normal pattern of evolution was interrupted by the construction, in the late 'fifties, of that giant out of her time, the GREAT EASTERN. Propelled by paddles and propeller, she was underpowered and a commercial failure. Her great size, over

The GREAT EASTERN, built on the Thames in 1854-58, had a top speed of about 14 knots and remained the world's largest vessel until 1899. This gigantic ship was launched broadside. PEREIRE, launched in November 1865, is seen below.

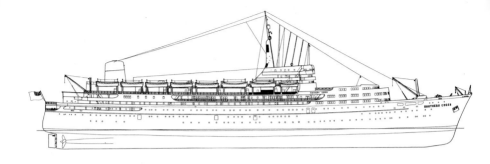

18,000 tons, remained unequalled for several decades.

The development of passenger ships during the nineteenth century is well shown by that of contemporary White Star Line vessels. Their pioneer steamer, the OCEANIC of 1870, was the first incidentally to have first-class accommodation amidships. She had a tonnage of 3,700, yet by 1899 that fleet was headed by a new OCEANIC of over 17,000 tons. The introduction of the compound engine nearly halved fuel consumption, and applied to the AGAMEMNON class of 1865 made it possible for Alfred Holt to make a success of his new service to the East. Soon, however, this type gave way to even more

The development of the passenger liner is shown here in the White Star OCEANIC of 1899 (bottom) and the SOUTHERN CROSS of 1955, the first of her type to have engines right aft.

efficient triple- and quadruple-expansion machinery.

The period from 1899 to 1914 saw a vast growth in the size of passenger ships, climaxed by Germany's three-funnelled VATERLAND of 1914, measuring over 54,000 tons gross. The era of the steam turbine came in with a rush. In 1907, only ten years after its first public demonstration, the LUSITANIA and MAURETANIA, the largest and fastest of their time, were so fitted. Today the world's largest passenger ship is the 83,000 ton QUEEN ELIZABETH, while for speed the UNITED STATES is likely to remain unequalled. However, nothing is static and the SOUTHERN CROSS of 1955 introduced a new concept, that of the ship devoted entirely to passengers, with no cargo space whatsoever.

For about a century, of all merchant ship types, it was the fast passenger liner which represented the peak of the naval architect's skill. But for every such vessel there were many smaller cargo ships, either tramps with large holds suited for bulk cargoes, or cargo liners designed for regular service on a particular trade. For these latter several internal decks were necessary, since much of their cargo was made up of separate consignments bound for a range of different ports.

A satisfactory method for the carriage of oil in bulk was only evolved after much experimentation and difficulty. The 2,300 ton GLÜCKAUF of 1886 is generally accepted as the prototype of the present giant tanker. Early this century their size outstripped longitudinal strength, so until a new system of longitudinal framing was developed there was a temporary reversion to the placing of engines amidships, even at the risk of increasing the fire hazard. The turret ship, in vogue at the turn of the century, was designed to take advantage of contemporary Suez Canal tonnage rules and charges. The peculiar cross section, with narrow top deck, also made these vessels very useful for high density cargoes. With her elaborate cargo gear and engines aft, the GRÄNGESBERG was an unusually sophisticated ship of her day, the forbear of the latest giant bulk carriers.

Although most of the early motorships were built in Russia, they were mainly small tankers for domestic trade and it was a Danish firm which first really developed the diesel engine into something suited for ocean-going vessels. Likewise, Danish and Swedish owners were the first to adopt the diesel for regular use. Perhaps to emphasize their difference, these early motorships had no funnels, only exhausts, but now the funnel is almost universal, an eye-catching feature which besides its main function often houses many items of equipment. For a ship to have reciprocating machinery is now a sign of age, the modern prime movers being the diesel or steam turbine. For merchant ships the gas turbine has not come up to expectation, while nuclear power still remains too costly to be justified for anything but naval and special purpose vessels such as icebreakers.

Latterly the trend has been for much higher speeds, and many fruiters and cargo liners now average over 20 knots. On the latter cargo handling gear has become much more elaborate, often including patent design masts such as the Hallén and Stülcken, the last named in association with very heavy lift derricks. The war-built standard ships of tramp type have come to the end of their economic life and the next few years will bring an interesting range of new designs to take their place.

The old concept of a passenger ship has changed to one of a vessel used mainly or entirely for cruising. However, the needs of the motorist have brought a fresh type into being — the ferry — which combines most

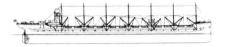

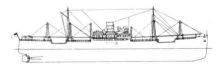

The 6,749 ton turret steamer GRÄNGES-BERG, built in 1903 to carry ore from Sweden to Holland, and (below) the New Zealand Line's OTAIO, of 1930, a refrigerated meat carrier of 10,048 tons.

of the features of a small passenger liner with drive-on facilities for large numbers of cars and other road vehicles. The transport of newly manufactured cars, often a thousand at a time, has resulted in another new type. Yet another new idea, developed from the wartime Landing Ship Dock, is a large vessel which carries its cargo in barges which, after being floated aboard through a stern opening, are stowed away by the ship's own cargo gear. So, among surface merchant vessels, the present picture is one of ever increasing variety, specialisation and automation. For tankers and bulk carriers the era of the giants is truly being ushered in. Even this is not all, for after years of development the hydrofoil and hovercraft are coming into their own for fast passenger work, the latter being particularly versatile since it is not confined to water but can travel equally well over icefield, swamp and land.

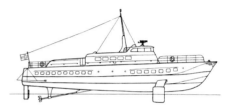

The short and the long of it: The Baltic hydrofoil SIRENA has a maximum of 40 knots, takes under three hours for passage from Stockholm to Mariehamn. The cargo liner ANDORRA does 18 knots, but her voyage between Copenhagen and Far Eastern ports takes two months each way.

On the following pages a collection of ship history—from early Viking longship to modern nuclear ship—is shown in full-colour drawings.

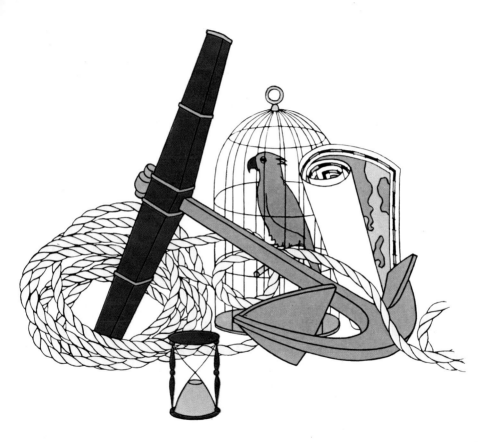

NORDIC VIKING SHIP, 10TH CENTURY

Built of oak and without decks, the Viking ships varied in size from small and intermediate types to the big men-of-war called "longships". Others, as is well known, made long ocean voyages, even across the Atlantic. This vessel is of the intermediate type (karvi) and generally similar to the Norwegian Gokstad ship. She measured about 77 ft. in length, 17 ft. in breadth and almost 6 ft. in depth. Such vessels could sail surprisingly close to the wind.

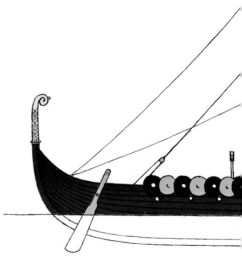

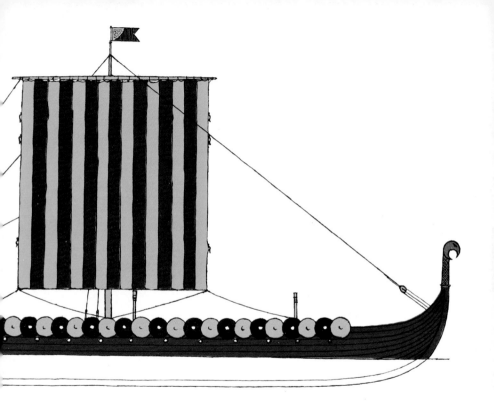

NORDIC KNARR, MID-13TH CENTURY

With the end of the Viking Era new shapes were being evolved, influenced by the ships of Western Europe and the Hanseatic League. The type known as cog now became common, displacing the older Nordic types. The knarr, or early cog (right) had the same rig and steering oar plus built-up castles forward and aft, as well as a fighting top. Sea warfare mainly involved boarding and hand-to-hand fighting, so even for merchantmen height brought advantages.

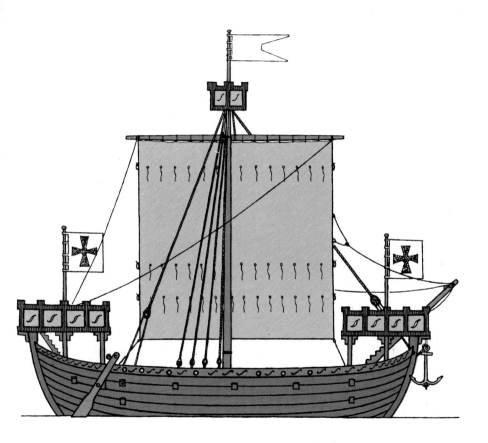

NORTH EUROPEAN HOLK, 15TH CENTURY

The cog, which was the large ship of the middle ages, was gradually replaced by the holk, which during the 15th century became the most important type in Northern Europe. The mizzen sail was borrowed from the Mediterranean lateen and aided steering. The rudder was another new feature, as were the detachable lower sails, called bonnets, which were a useful substitute for reefing. The castles, too, had evolved into an integral part of the hull.

WEST EUROPEAN CARRACK, 16TH CENTURY

Found in the Mediterranean and in Western Europe, the carrack was probably developed in Italy. Genoa used carracks from the fifteenth century for her trade with England, although the earliest ones were single-masted. The vessel shown has a bonnet to each lower sail, while above the fighting tops extra sails—topsails— are carried. Unlike those shown previously, which were clinker-built i.e. with overlapping planks, carracks had carvel, or flush surface hulls.

PINNACE, ABOUT 1650

The pinnace, a new type developed in Holland at the beginning of the 17th century, differed from the earlier flute in having a beakhead and a square transom. As men-of-war, pinnaces could carry about 24 guns between decks; and some, used as merchantmen, made long voyages. As seen opposite, the transom was kept low; above it the stern carried an allegorical painting representing the ship's name. In contrast, the English pinnace was a small boat with oars and sail, of a type often carried by men-of-war.

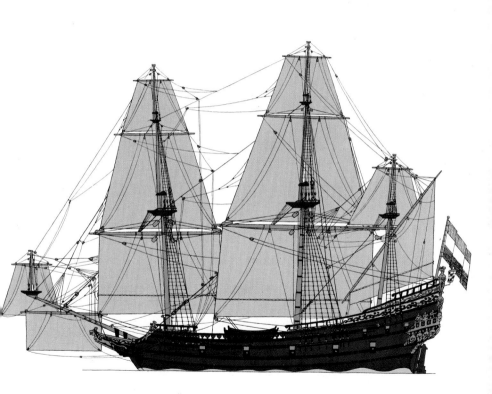

SWEDISH MAIL PACKET, 1692

While sailing ships of all sizes were being built to an ever increasing upper size limit, a multitude of special service craft were designed to meet local requirements. The Swedish postal department used a number of vessels like the HIORTEN to carry the mails, passengers and light cargo. Rated as a sloop—then a vessel with only one deck —she was built at Karlskrona and operated between Ystad and Stralsund until 1702.

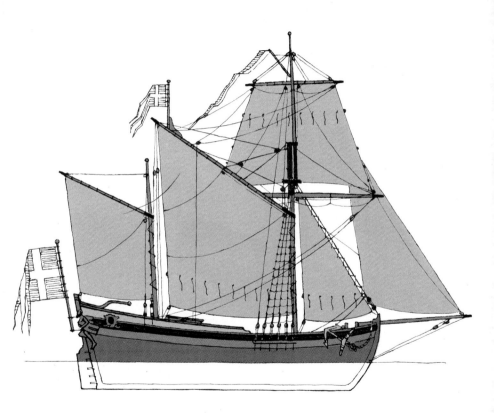

DUTCH SLOOP, 1678

If used for official purposes a vessel of this type was known as a Statenjacht. Another, owned perhaps by a wealthy merchant and used as a pleasure yacht, was called a Speeljacht. Like all shallow draught Dutch craft, the sloop had a hinged lee-board on each side. When sailing close to the wind the one on the lee side would be lowered to provide a better grip in the water and so prevent the vessel from drifting too far down wind.

GÖTA LEJON 1746

This Swedish ship-of-the-line which mounted 72 guns was built at Karlskrona by Gilbert Sheldon. She had a remarkably long career and was 44 years old when she took part in the Swedish war with Russia, including the battle in which the Swedish Navy broke out of Viborg. She was finally scrapped in 1816, when 70 years old.

39

SWEDISH EAST INDIAMAN, 1768

The Swedish East India Company was established in 1731, 131 years after its British counterpart, and existed until 1813. Altogether it owned 38 ships which made about 130 voyages to the Far East. The GÖTHEBORG, right, was the largest yet built for the fleet and could carry 530 lasts, or loads, one last being equal to 2.5 tons d.w. She mounted a large number of guns and but for her fuller lines resembled a frigate.

41

STOCKHOLMSHÄXAN 1816

In Europe, Sweden was second only to Britain in steamboat construction, much work being done by an English settler, Samuel Owen. A believer in screw propulsion, he converted a Lake Malar sloop, giving her a single cylinder 4 h.p. engine and a 5 ft. diameter screw with four wooden blades. She achieved 4 knots but her boiler, as expected, was too small for sustained use. Shortly afterwards Owen built two more successful steamboats.

43

BALTIMORE CLIPPER, 1820

After the 1812 war with Britain, certain American shipbuilders began to construct faster vessels, schooners and brigs, which engaged in the most profitable of the world's trades. Mainly built in Virginia and Maryland, these small, beamy craft were known throughout the world as Baltimore clippers. Rigged as a two-topsail schooner and carrying a great spread of canvas, this vessel had a very raked stem and maximum draft aft. She mounted four small guns on each side.

CURAÇAO 1825

Launched as the CALPE, this paddle steamer was originally intended for service between England, North America and the West Indies. However, in 1826 she was bought by the Netherlands and renamed CURAÇAO, to become the first steam vessel in the Dutch Navy. Prior to 1830 she made three trans-Atlantic voyages to South America and the West Indies, carrying passengers, mails and valuable cargo. Then for some years she traded in European waters, afterwards returning to the West Indies. She was withdrawn from service in 1846 and four years later was sold for scrap.

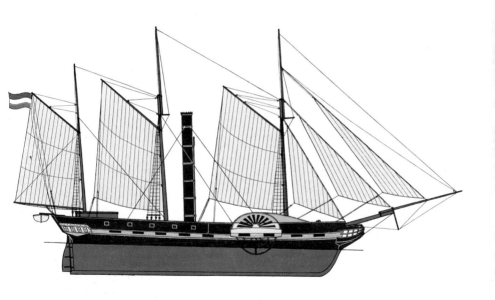

BRITANNIA 1840

The first of the original quartette built for Mr. Samuel Cunard's famous trans-Atlantic service, this 1,156 ton ship could accommodate 115 passengers and carry 225 tons of cargo. She and her sisters ACADIA, CALEDONIA and COLUMBIA provided fortnightly sailings between Liverpool, Halifax and Boston. She was 207 ft. long, had 2-cylinder, side-lever machinery and four boilers working at 9 p.s.i. In 1849, after 40 Atlantic crossings she was sold to become a German warship.

GREAT BRITAIN 1843

The first screw steamer built for trans-Atlantic service, she was designed by Isambard Kingdom Brunel for the Great Western Steamship Company. Built of iron in a dry dock at Bristol, she measured 289 ft. × 50 ft. and could accommodate 360 passengers. After two years on the Atlantic she foundered off Ireland, but was re-floated, sold and re-engined. After further trading to America and Australia she was converted into a sailing ship. Her hull still exists in South Georgia, "down under" in the near-Polar regions of the South Atlantic.

HANSINE 1850

This long-lived vessel was built of oak at Schleswig. Originally named HANSINE, she became the HANSINA in 1896, when sold to a Swedish owner at Simrishamn. Subsequently owned in other ports, she was scrapped in the early 1930s. To be technically correct she should be described as a topgallant schooner since she carries a topgallant-sail over her topsail. However, such vessels were familiarly referred to as topsail schooners, even though this implied the presence of a topsail only.

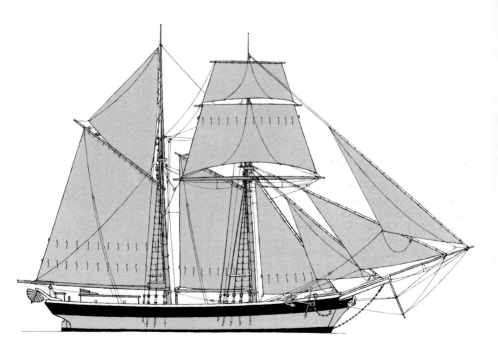

COMMONWEALTH 1854

Typical of the many steamboats used for night services between ports on America's Eastern rivers and sounds, the COMMONWEALTH had 120 two-berth cabins, with open berthing for another 600 passengers. Luxuriously fitted out, she plied between New York and Norwich, and later to Groton, until 1865, when both terminal and ship were destroyed by fire. Her hull measured 300 ft. x 41.5 ft., but her breadth on deck was 77 ft. She had a vertical beam engine and two boilers.

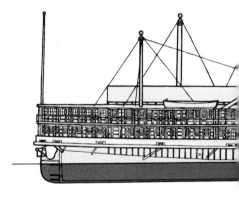

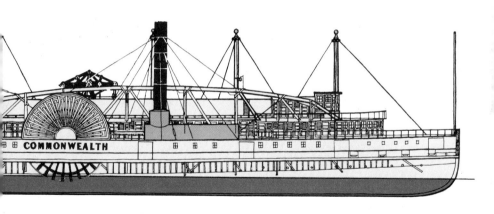

ADRIATIC 1856

*This luxuriously appointed vessel of 3,670
tons was built for the Collins Line's New
York-Liverpool trade and could accommodate 366 passengers. She was the last
Atlantic liner built with a wooden hull
and measured 344 ft. × 50 ft. Her normal
speed was 13 knots. She made only two
voyages before her owner's short-lived service
closed down. Briefly owned by the Galway
Line, she then became a sailing ship.
She was condemned in 1885.*

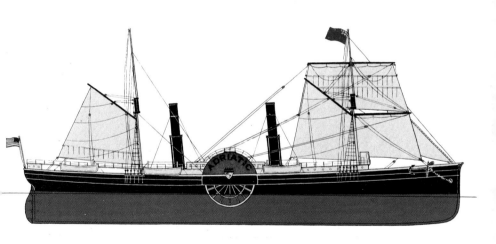

PERSISTANT 1865

Besides the large ocean-going sailers and small coastal vessels, there were many others of medium size which were used on the more extended coastal routes and on the shorter ocean trades—in fact the ancestors of today's short sea traders. Such a vessel was the PERSISTANT, a French barque of 445 tons net, which was built at Nantes, with a wooden hull which measured 145 ft. × 30 ft. Throughout her career she was owned at Le Havre, until 1893 when her name was removed from the register.

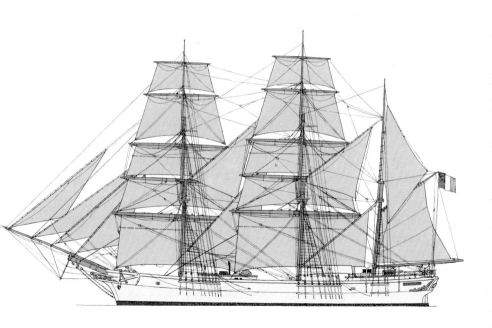

CITY OF PARIS 1865

*On the North Atlantic route the Inman
Line had an excellent reputation with passengers, although their ships were not
generally fliers. Their 2,556 ton CITY OF
PARIS, a 13-knot, iron-hulled ship, was
originally fitted with two-cylinder horizontal trunk engines of 2,600 i.h.p. using
steam at 30 p.s.i. In 1871 she was lengthened
from 346 ft. to 398 ft. and was later
given compound machinery. Sold in 1883,
she was sunk in collision two years later as
the French TONQUIN.*

GREAT REPUBLIC 1866

Ponderous of profile although slim-lined, this 3,881-ton trans-Pacific liner was one of a quartette built for the Pacific Mail Steamship Co. For eight years she and the AMERICA, CHINA and JAPAN maintained a monthly service with great regularity. The largest commercial steamers to have wooden hulls, they were propelled by vertical beam engines. The GREAT REPUBLIC measured 360 ft. × 47 ft. and could accommodate 250 cabin and 1,200 steerage passengers.

NATCHEZ 1869

*Famed for her million dollar race of 1870
with the ROBERT E. LEE, this Mississippi
packet had the shallow, beamy hull traditional
for this type. Her length was 303 ft. and her
breadth on the waterline 46 ft., but overhang
increased the deck width to 83 ft. Against the
current she could do 18 knots; with it—on
occasion—25 knots. Cargo was piled high on
the main deck, while above there was elaborately embellished passenger accommodation.*

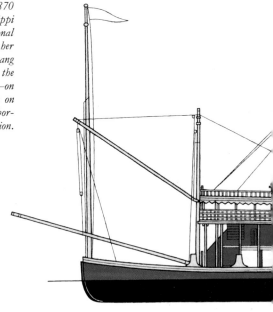

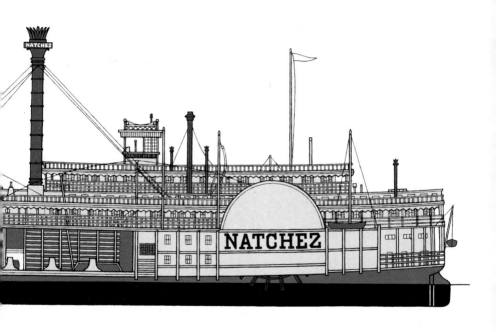

NORMAN COURT 1869

One of the later British tea clippers, she was built in the same year as the famous CUTTY SARK. London-owned and of 834 tons net, she had a composite hull 200 ft. long overall and 33 ft. in breadth. Several years on the China trade were followed by a period of alternating voyages to Australia and China. In 1881, three years after being re-rigged as a barque, she was wrecked near Holyhead.

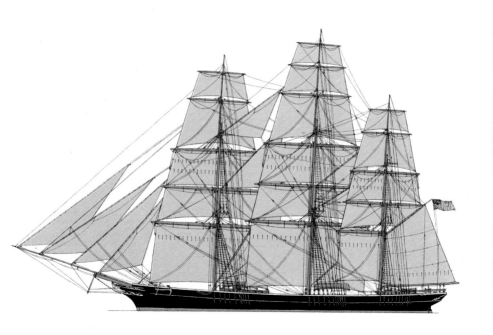

ORIENT 1879

Built for the Orient Line by John Elder & Company, Glasgow, this 5,386 ton, iron-hulled steamer measured 445 ft. × 46 ft. She carried up to 550 passengers and with the GREAT EASTERN was one of the largest ships afloat. Compound machinery gave a trial speed of 17 knots. This very popular ship was rebuilt in 1899 with only one funnel and two masts. In 1909 she was withdrawn and was scrapped the following year.

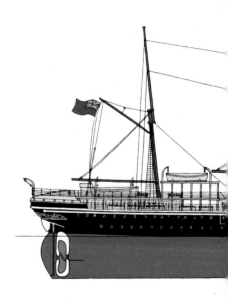

GLÜCKAUF 1886

The accepted prototype of the present tanker, this 2,307 ton steamer was built by Armstrong, Whitworth & Co. for the Deutsche Amerikanische Petroleum Gesellschaft. Her iron and steel hull measured 300 ft. × 37 ft. and had centreline and transverse bulkheads. A fore and aft expansion tank placed between her two decks was flanked by tanks for lighter oils. She operated with success until 1893, when she stranded near New York.

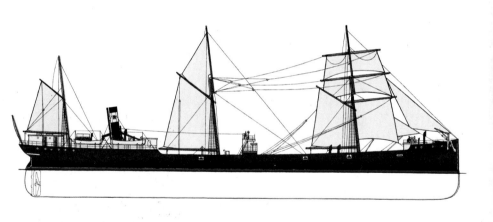

POTOSI 1895

The nitrate sailers owned by F. Laeisz of Hamburg were world-famous for their size and strength. Built by Tecklenborg of Geestemünde, the POTOSI, 4,026 tons, measured 366 ft. × 49 ft. and was the world's largest five-masted barque. Under the German flag she made 28 round voyages to Chile via the Horn and proved capable of 17 knots. In 1925, as the Chilean-owned FLORA, she was lost by fire in the South Atlantic.

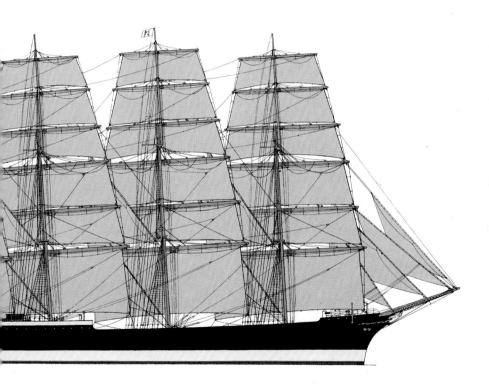

KAISER WILHELM DER GROSSE
1897

*By winning the Blue Riband this 14,349
ton ship put the Norddeutscher Lloyd in
a prime position in Atlantic shipping.*
*Built at Stettin, she was 627 ft. long and
could accommodate over 1,600 passengers
in three classes. Giant quadruple expansion
engines of 28,000 i.h.p. gave her a
speed of over 22 knots. Her New York
service ended with the 1914 war. A few
weeks later, while acting as a commerce
raider, she was sunk by the British cruiser
HIGHFLYER.*

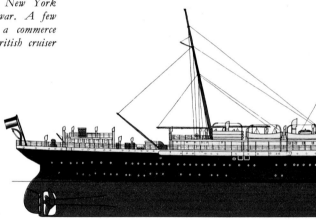

COCKERILL 1901

One of the multitude of small cargo steamers which, on ocean routes, gradually supplanted the sailing vessel, the COCKERILL, of 2,441 tons, measured 288 ft. × 45 ft. She had reciprocating machinery and two Scotch boilers. A single deck ship, she had four bulkheads and hatches, the latter being served by seven derricks. Built and originally owned in Belgium by the Société Anonyme John Cockerill, she was torpedoed in 1917 as the British owned MABEL BAIRD.

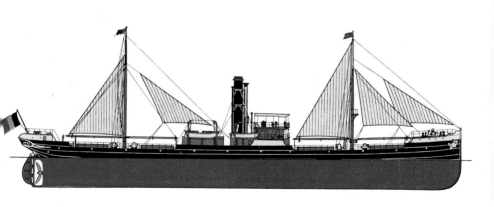

MOZART 1904

This four-masted barquentine was built at Greenock for German ownership. Her registered dimensions were 260 ft. × 40.5 ft. and she had a gross tonnage of 2,005. She was very up-to-date in design, and besides being fitted with water ballast tanks, she was given such labour-saving devices as halliard and brace winches, steam-powered by a donkey boiler.

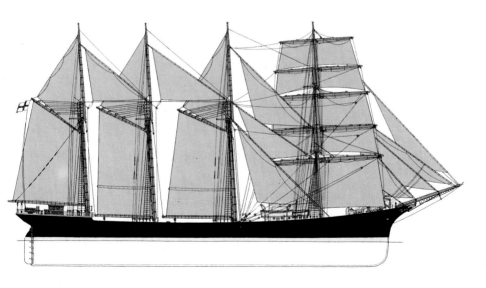

ARCHIBALD RUSSELL 1905

The fortunes of the deep-sea sailing ship were in steep decline when this vessel was launched, and she was the last four-masted barque to be built for British owners. Steel-hulled and of 2,385 tons gross, she measured 278 ft. × 43 ft. Built at Greenock for John Hardie & Co., Glasgow, she remained with them until 1924 when she was sold to Finland. She was damaged during the 1939 war, and scrapped a few years later.

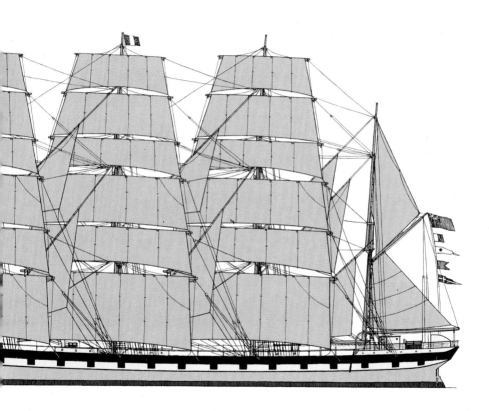

MAURETANIA 1907

*Built for the Cunard Line, on the Tyne
and Clyde respectively, she and the
LUSITANIA were the first turbine-
driven express liners and they outpaced all
others on the North Atlantic. The LUS-
ITANIA was torpedoed in 1915, but the
MAURETANIA—slightly the faster
—held the Blue Riband until 1929. Six
years later she was scrapped. Her gross
tonnage was 31,938 and machinery of
70,000 s.h.p. (shaft horse power) gave her
a trial speed of 27.4 knots.*

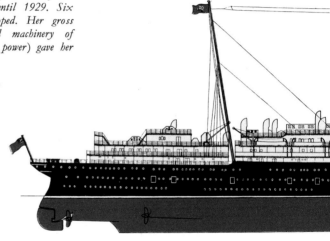

WILLAPA 1908

From the mid-nineteenth century, timber from the north Californian coast was carried south by sailing vessels which loaded on a stormy coast virtually devoid of shelter. The steamers which followed were likewise known as Redwood schooners. Typical of these, the 752-ton WILLAPA, owned at San Francisco, had a hull of Douglas fir measuring 178 ft. × 40 ft. and an engine of 475 i.h.p. She foundered off the Honduran Coast in 1916.

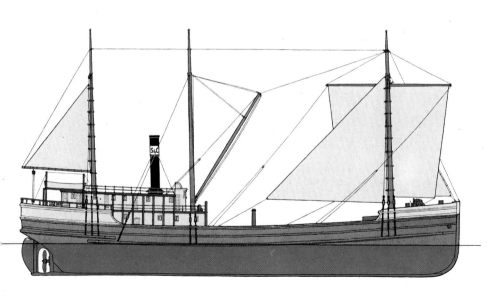

SELANDIA 1912

The first ocean-going cargo liner to be diesel driven, the SELANDIA, 4,950 gross tonnage, proved an outstanding success. Built and engined by Burmeister & Wain, Copenhagen, she had two 8-cylinder, 4-stroke single-acting diesels, each of 1,250 h.p. Owned by the East Asiatic Company, Copenhagen, she carried up to 24 passengers and operated on the Bangkok service. She was sold in 1936 to become the NORSEMAN, and was wrecked in 1942 as the Finnish-owned TORNATOR.

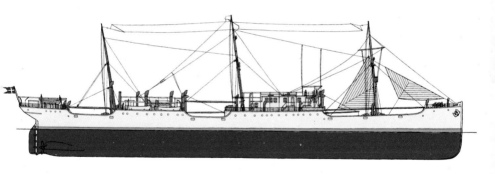

JAN PIETERSZOON COEN 1915

This 15 knot, 11,692-ton liner was built at Amsterdam for the Nederlandsche Stoomvaart Maatschappij for their East Indies trade and had accommodation for over 400 passengers, including 202 first class. Her five holds were served by hydraulic cranes as well as derricks. She was 503 ft. long and had twin-screw, triple-expansion engines of 6,000 h.p. In 1940 she was scuttled off Ymuiden to block the entrance to the North Sea Canal.

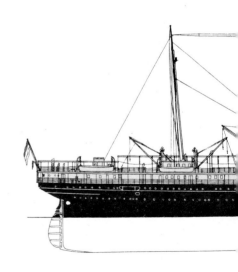

KAJ HVILSOM 1918

After the first world war very few sailing ships were built and in Europe the old sailing schooners soon gave way to auxiliary powered vessels—motor sailers, as they were often called. Of the traditional schooners which relied on sail alone, one of the last to be commissioned was the Danish KAJ HVILSOM. This wooden-hulled vessel was built at Svendborg for a local firm, the Rederi A/B Panis. Her registered dimensions were 137 ft. × 30 ft. and she had a net tonnage of 300. She was sold to Reval (later Tallinn) in 1926, but by 1929 her name had disappeared from the register.

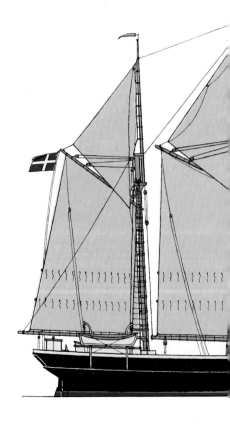

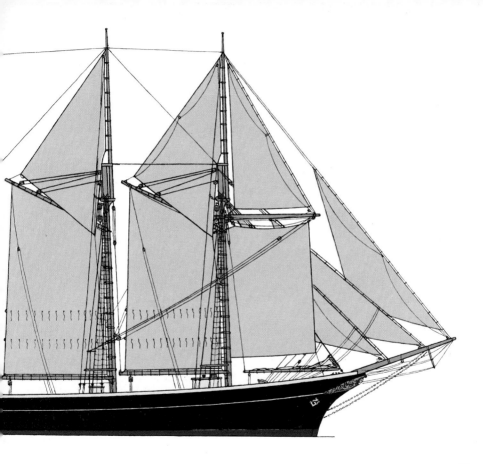

SAINT DUNSTAN 1919

This Tyne-built tramp steamer of 5,662 tons gross was typical of many built in Britain between the first world war and the mid-'thirties. She was 400 ft. long, had four main holds and reciprocating machinery giving a speed of 11 knots. She was never sold and remained with the Saint Line, Ltd., London—until sunk in the Atlantic by torpedo in August 1940.

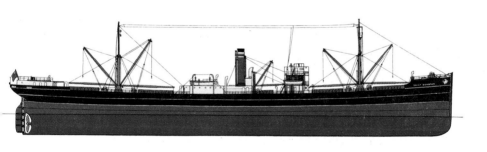

GRIPSHOLM 1925

Built for the Svenska Amerika Linien by Sir W. G. Armstrong, Whitworth & Co. Ltd., Newcastle, the GRIPSHOLM was the first North Atlantic passenger liner to be diesel-driven. Her two B. & W. engines—of an entirely new type—developed 13,500 h.p. and gave a speed of 17 knots. Her gross tonnage was 17,993 and she measured 553 ft. × 74 ft. Modernised after the war, she was later sold to the Norddeutscher Lloyd and as their BERLIN lasted until late 1966, when she was sold to Italian breakers.

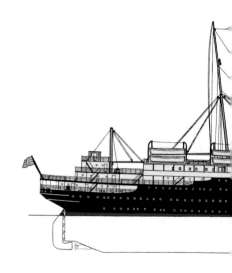

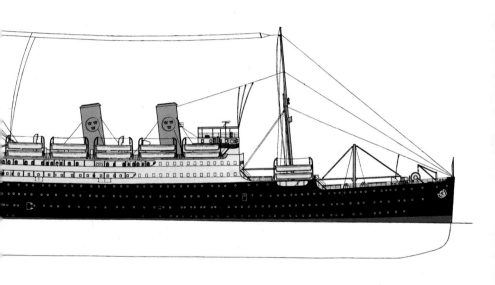

DAGNY 1926

The shapes of vessels frequently reveal national and sometimes even regional characteristics. This small Swedish schooner has the distinctive Marstal type of hull with square stern and nearly vertical stem. Ordered from the Ystad yard as a sailing ship, she was launched with an auxiliary diesel on board. Later, during the 'forties, the war caused many more auxiliary schooners to be built in Sweden, especially at Kalmar and Karlstad. These, however, had steel hulls.

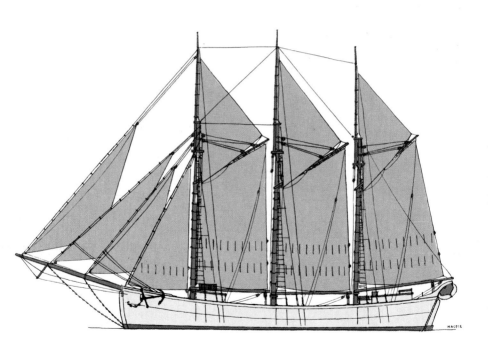

BREMEN 1928

This 51,565 ton Norddeutscher Lloyd liner in 1929 regained for Germany the Blue Riband lost for over 20 years. She was Bremen-built, though her sister EUROPA came from Hamburg. The BREMEN had eleven decks amidships, a bulbous bow, anti-rolling tanks and geared turbines of 123,000 h.p. Her best eastward average was 28.51 knots. She measured 898.7 ft. × 101.9 ft. and could carry nearly 3,000 passengers in four classes. In 1941 she was bombed and burnt out at Bremerhaven.

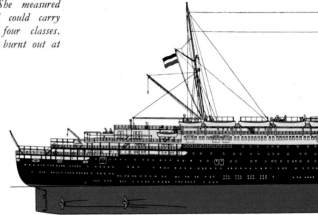

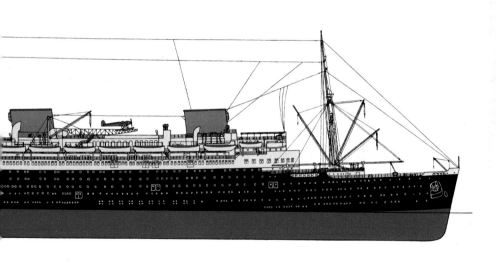

NORMANDIE 1932

The world's largest at her launching, she won the Blue Riband on her maiden voyage and did not finally lose it until 1938. On her best crossing she averaged 31.2 knots. Luxuriously appointed, the NOR-MANDIE could carry 1,975 passengers in seven classes. Of 83,432 tons gross, she measured 1,029 ft. (o.a.) × 118 ft. and had turbo-electric machinery of 160,000 h.p. Taken over later to become the American LAFAYETTE, she capsized after fire at New York in February 1942.

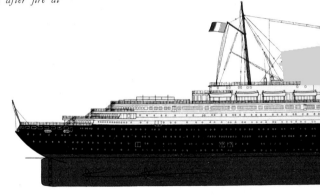

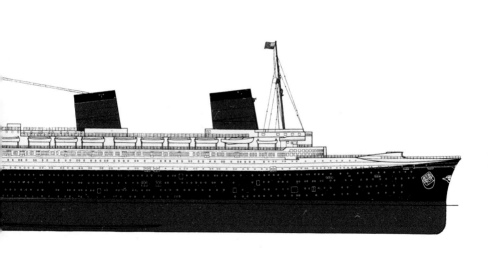

QUEEN MARY 1936

Her construction long suspended through the business depression, this 81,235 ton Cunard liner entered service in May 1936. Her early Atlantic record was soon bettered by the NORMANDIE, but in 1938 the QUEEN MARY—designed to average 29 knots—regained the Blue Riband with a crossing at 31.69 knots. Powered by turbines of 160,000 h.p., she measures 1,019 ft. × 119 ft. and carries up to 1,960 passengers in three classes. Her wartime troop capacity was 15,000 men.

ORANJE 1939

Owned by the Nederlandsche Stoomvaart Maatschappij, the 20,017 ton ORANJE was the world's fastest motor liner, three Sulzer diesels of 37,500 b.h.p. giving a top speed of 26 knots. She measured 656 ft. × 83 ft. and her hull was unique for its great amount of tumble-home, which reduced deck width to 66 ft. As built, she carried 740 passengers in four classes. Latterly used on around-the-world service, she was sold in 1964 and reconstructed to become the ANGELINA LAURO.

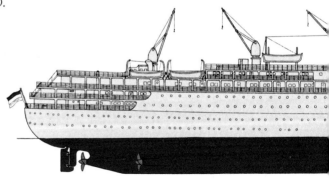

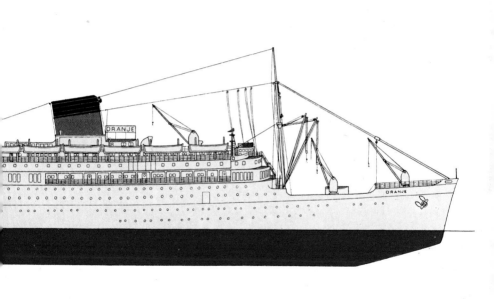

UNITED STATES 1952

This quadruple-screw liner is the present holder of the Atlantic Blue Riband. In 1952 she broke both records on her maiden voyage and averaged 35.59 knots eastwards. A ship of light construction, designed to meet Service requirements, her fittings are all either fire resisting or fire retarding. She measures 990 ft. (o.a.) × 102 ft. and carries up to 1,930 passengers. As built her gross tonnage was 53,329.

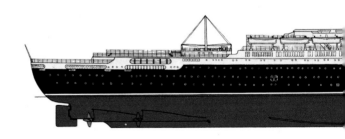

KISTA DAN 1952

One of a series of specialised ice-breaking cargo ships built for J. Lauritzen, Copenhagen, the KISTA DAN, 1,244 tons gross, measures 213 ft. × 37 ft. She has two holds and accommodation for 24 passengers. Her exceptionally strong hull has fins to deflect heavy ice from the screw and a horn for protection when going astern. On occasion she has served as an Antarctic supply vessel. In open water she has a speed of 12 knots.

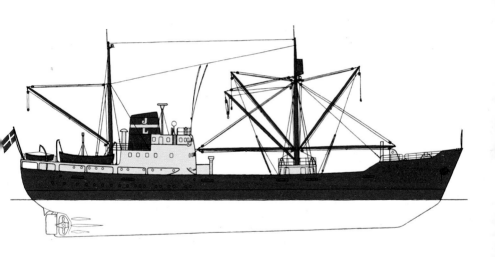

UNIVERSE APOLLO 1959

Of 72,133 tons gross, this giant tanker was the first to exceed the 100,000 ton mark. She was built in a drydock at Kure, Japan, for Universe Tankships Inc., Monrovia, one of the Ludwig Group. Her length is 950 ft. and breadth 135 ft. Geared turbines of 25,000 s.h.p. give a service speed of 15.5 knots. Four pumps, each of 1,000 h.p., can discharge her cargo in 30 hours. Her normal complement is 77 men.

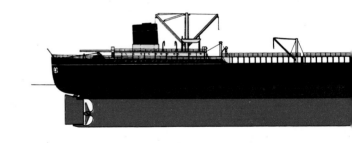

ROTTERDAM 1959

Designed both for North Atlantic service and cruising, this 38,645 ton Holland-America Line ship carries a maximum of 647 first and 809 tourist class passengers, but when cruising these are limited to 730 in one class. She measures 749 ft. × 94 ft., is stabilised and air-conditioned and has geared turbines of 17,300 h.p. which give her a service speed of 20.5 knots.

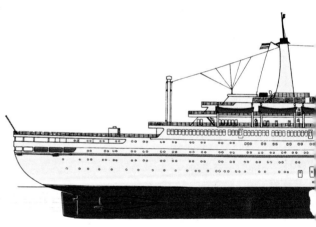

SAVANNAH 1962

*The world's first commercial nuclear ship,
the 15,585 ton SAVANNAH was built at
Camden, N. J. Designed for demonstration
purposes, she was not expected to be com-
mercially competitive. In 1965, after a
series of demonstration voyages, she was
for a time employed on a regular European
cargo service. She measures 595 ft. × 78 ft.
and has seven holds. Her single set of
turbines, taking steam from a reactor
placed forward of the bridge, gives her a
speed of 20 knots.*

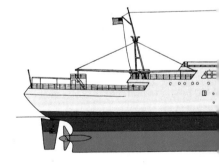

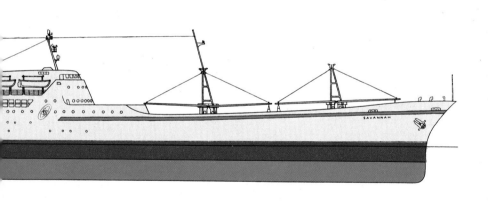

AMERICAN CHALLENGER 1962

*The first of an 11-ship class of express
cargo liners for the United States Lines,
she has a service speed of 21 knots. She is
560 ft. long, 75 ft. in breadth and has a
gross tonnage of 11,185. Of her six holds,
two have triple hatches abreast and one
of her derricks is of 70 tons capacity. Her
geared turbines develop a maximum of
18,150 h.p.*

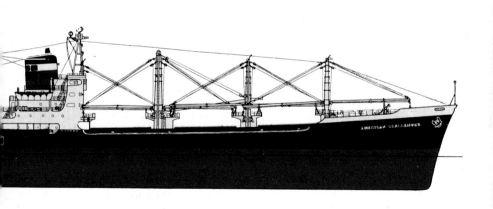

FLANDRIA 1964

Built within the framework of regulations which give economic advantages to a ship of 499 tons gross over one of 500, the FLANDRIA is one of the so-called "paragraph boats". She is 248 ft. long, of 499 tons gross and has side doors, three decks and two holds. Most of her cargo, including pallets and containers, is handled by fork lift trucks. She was designed to trade between Gothenburg, her home port, and Antwerp.

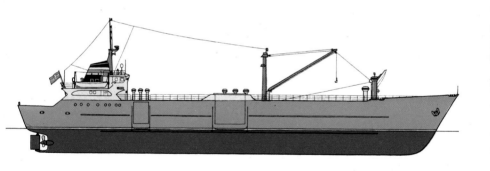

EMMA MAERSK 1964

Once considered large, but now hardly so, this tanker of 36,440 tons gross was built and engined by Kockums, Malmo. for A. P. Moller, of Copenhagen. She measures 775 ft. × 109 ft. and geared turbines give a loaded speed of 17 knots. Her cargo space is divided by two longitudinal bulkheads and comprises 19 tanks. A special feature is the automatic bridge control of the engines. Later, larger tankers generally have their bridge located aft.

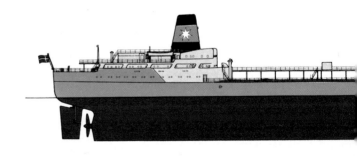

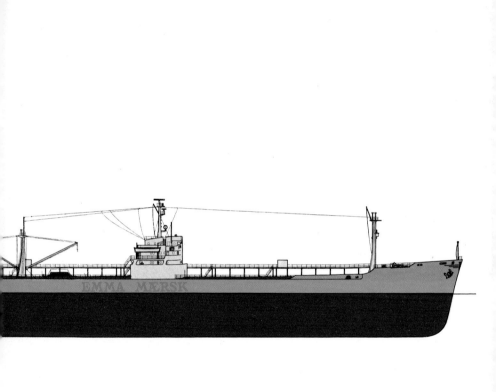

BERGECHIEF 1964

When completed in 1964 the BERGE-CHIEF, of 92,420 tons deadweight, was the largest motor tanker ever built in Norway, indeed anywhere in the world. She is practically all welded and measures 869 ft. × 122 ft. Her cargo space is divided by two longitudinal and many transverse bulkheads into 25 tanks. She was built at Stavanger by the Rosenberg Mekaniske Verksted A/S for Sig. Bergesen Junior & Co., also of Stavanger. In 1967 several much larger Bergesen tankers were under construction in Norway and Japan, including two each of 191,000 tons deadweight.

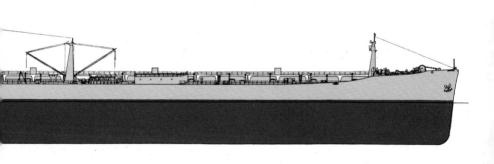

SAGA 1966

Built and engined by the Lindholmens Varv. for the Swedish Lloyd, this 7,889 ton, 18 knot ship can accommodate 408 passengers and has drive-on facilities for 100 cars and 106 freight containers. One of three which maintain the England-Sweden Line's North Sea services, she operates to Tilbury, the others to Hull. She is stabilised, measures 463 ft. × 69 ft. and has twin screws driven by two pairs of diesels totalling 10,800 h.p.

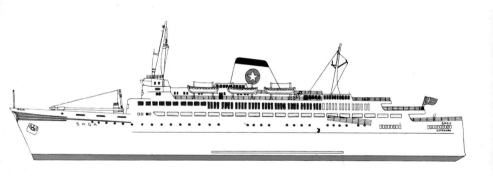

OLD SAILING-SHIP OWNERS' HOUSE FLAGS

A

1. The Hanseatic League, Lübeck (The middle ages)
2. The East India Company, London
3. Black Ball Line, New York (1816)
4. Enoch Train White Diamond Line, Boston, Mass. (1820's)
5. Grinnell, Minturn & Co, New York, Swallow Tail Line to Liverpool
6. Grinnell, Minturn & Co, New York, Swallow Tail Line to London
7. Arthur Sewall, Bath, Me.
8. Alaska Packers Association, San Francisco
9. Money Wigram & Sons, London
10. George Thompson & Co, Aberdeen White Star Line, Aberdeen
11. John Willis & Son, London
12. Devitt & Moore, London
13. John Hardie & Co, Glasgow
14. Thomas Law & Co, Shire Line, Glasgow
15. John Stewart & Co, London
16. Andrew Weir & Co, Bank Line, Glasgow
17. Soc. Anon. des Voiliers Nantais, Nantes
18. Ferdinand Laeisz, Hamburg
19. S. O. Stray & Co, Kristiansand
20. Gustaf Erikson, Mariehamn

B

Other house marks:

A number of companies had other signs of recognition than their flags. These markings can be compared with the funnel markings used nowadays. The Black Ball Line of New York had, for example, a black ball on the fore topsail.

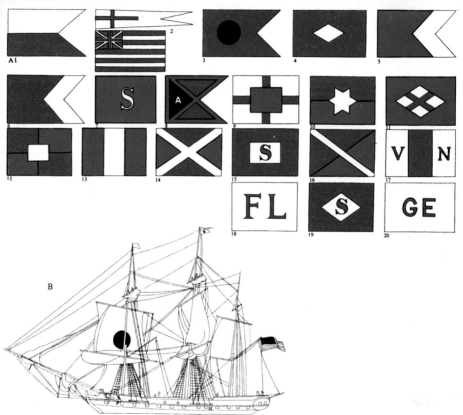